INTRODUCTION

An ironic unveiling of an individual at the mercy of a system that could become cold and mechanical, *Anatomy of an Illness* is a personal point of view of a collective experience, regardless that the diagnosis is AIDS, Cancer or a heart attack.

This fragmented text- a hybrid between poetry and theater- is the result of the mixture of heartbreaking hours of insomnia in the hospital bed and readings from magazines, spiritual books, and pamphlets for patients. Also from entries of the author's personal diary at transformational retreats and from her notes commenting on posters and television programs watched at treatment centers' waiting rooms. Like a scrapbook made out mementos. All is seamlessly blended to create a distillation born on the process of healing from a deadly disease.

Anatomy of an Illness presents a metaphor of illness as a battle of the body pitched against itself as part of the war versus True Self.

Maitreyi Villamán-Matos

Anatomy Of an Illness

Maitreyi Villamán Matos

Anatomy of an Illness premiered as a performance, and was simultaneously released as a book on October 6, 2011 in Charlottesville, VA at Chroma Project - Art Laboratory

A performance of *Anatomy of an Illness* was filmed by Calvin Tate and can be viewed at of Charlottesville Public Access Television or at LaMagaScene.org, LaMagaPress.org and CentroInarú.org.

Copyright© 2011 by Maitreyi Villamán Matos
All rights reserved. No parts of this publication may be reproduced or transmitted in any form or any means, without permission in writing from the publisher.

Design and Publisher: Mercedes A. Villamán
Proof reader: Sheri Grupp

ISBN-13: 978-0615540900
Published in United States of America, by La Maga Press. 416 E. Main Street, Suite 301C, Charlottesville, VA 22902 lamagapress@gmail.com

Tel. 434-981-5770 - La Maga Press/Facebook

To my Guru,

Sri Swami Satchidananda Maharaj.

To my mother, Francisca Diaz Matos.

To my sisters, Chayo, and Ama;

To Marién, Morganna, Roberto, and Eric.

And to Jeff Fogel, for being such a good friend.

Anatomy of an Illness

"Just bear in mind that sickness is the means by which an organism frees itself from what is alien."

Rainer Maria Rilke
Letters to a Young Poet

Just for today:
I am grateful.
I release
All anger and resentment.
I release
All worry and fear.
I live and work
With mindfulness and with Integrity.
I show loving kindness and compassion to myself and All beings.

Terri Osborne (The Five Precepts)

UNIVERSAL PRAYER

THE LIGHT OF GOD SURROUNDS US

THE LOVE OF GOD ENFOLDS US

THE POWER OF GOD PROTECTS US

THE PRESENCE OF GOD WATCHES US

WHEREVER WE ARE…

GOD IS…

AND ALL IS WELL!

The sea does not

reward those who

are too anxious, too

greedy, or too
impatient.

One should lay empty,

open,

Choiceless

as a beach waiting for a
gift
from the sea.

Anne Morrow Lindberg

The **patient's robe** puts me into a world of questioning

The hospital entrance required an abandonment of the self-will, a nakedness of identities and a surrender of the personal story, showing the non- physical aspect of our illness. In the bathroom, unfolding the clothes that attach me to the regular passenger in the medical records, the nurse had placed in my hand a gown of questioning, and asked me to put it on.

Naked already as I am, the hospital bathroom light shines upon **my skinny body**, and bruised skin, the rope that will set the pace of the non- physical aspect of my illness.

WE ARE READY FOR YOU

I feel the journey of ten names,

two thousand lifetimes.

This moment is calling.

I will ask this moment to leave a message;

I am not here at this moment.

The past has claimed my soul in a dance

of memories,

bubbling up gentle crystal clear images,

guarantying a private heaven of a devilish

dance.

And these bubbles of memories

expanding within

are taking their place, enthroning

themselves in a seat of shame.

Innocent, the air is a mist covering the taste of the moonlight like a distant echo, like a spider web of invisible threads, tied, holding captive, capturing the soul to an insufficiency and these bubbles of images are traitors bursting, in happy explosions of sounds to the gentle touch of the deepest darkness.

Here, with half naked body in an insufficient plead of misery,

I AM AT THE TOTAL MERCY OF STRANGERS, my regular clothes gathered on the clean hospital floor, the present peels off the reality. My clothes are without life or purpose, a distant mask, of solitude, **and the nurse, all ten fingers of precision** imposing on this naked body the reality of my own journey, as the new garment that she slips up my arms in a wave, pale color of sickness. A small print among the hospital paintings is looking at me from the reclining bed, illness takes hold of nine years of denial, a bed that maybe I had helped to make.

I I í ı ı ı í ı̂ í í í í í

l i i i i ì i i i i

Me Me Me me me me me me

my my my my my my

my í i i i i i

ℐ ℐ ℐ ℐ ℐ ℐ ℐ ℐ ℐ ℐ ME ME
ME ME ME ME ME ME
ME MY MY MY MY MY
MY MY *I I I I I I I I*
I I I I I I I I I ME ME
ME ME ME ME ME ME
ME MY MY MY MY MY

MY MY I I I I I I I I I I
I I I I I I ME ME ME ME
ME ME ME ME ME MY
MY MY MY MY MY MY *i*
iiiiiiiiiiiiiiii ME ME ME

ME ME ME ME ME ME *my*

my my my my my my ℐ ℐ ℐ ℐ
ℐ ℐ ℐ ℐ ℐ ℐ ℐ ℐ ℐ ℐ ME ME
ME ME ME ME ME ME
ME

my my my my my my my
ii
iiiiiiiiiiiiiii ME ME ME
ME ME ME ME ME ME
MY MY MY MY MY MY
MY ℐℐℐℐℐℐℐℐℐℐℐℐℐℐℐ
ME ME ME ME ME ME *me me*

Me My My My
My my my my I I I I
I I I I I I I I I I I I I
Me Me Me me Me me Me me Me
My My My My My my my I I
I I I I I I I I I I I I I
I Me Me Me me

me me me me me my my my
my my my my I I I I I I I I
I I I I I I I I Me Me Me me
me me me me me my my my my my my
my I I I I I I I I I I I I I

I I I I Me Me Me me me me me
me me my my my my my my my I I I
I I I I I I I I I I I I I I I
Me Me Me me me me me me me my
my my my my my my **I I I I I I -**

**Ay – ay – ay –
ay- ay-ay-ay i i i
i i ay- ay-ay-ay-
ay-ay-ay** I me my

Ay mi mai!

"Now I do not feel that good when I see the heartbreaks you embrace. If I were a master thief…I'd rob them".

Lyrics from a Bob Dylan song

A labyrinth across the map of
the fake reality of the mind
winding up and down in
intertwining patterns of
thoughts. Sometimes like a
spiral, this journey takes on a
familiar face
and can be said to be the same
old song,
with just a tiny improvement in
the melody.
But the spiral never passes the
same place,
the trace going in concentric
movement toward the center.
 The geometric shape is drawing
a line of destiny, away from
itself.

Collaboration is the key

Collaboration is something like a mystery

A partnership.

More like a friendship

And getting comfortable takes time,

Beating the symptoms

Me, a patient lying down the mind

in a cozy room with a view.

A tree dressing the window,

And this offer is just for you!

Cut Your Mom Some Slack

 In the mind, it's important to draw the characters in perspective. As you rest in the hospital, a corpse bleeding on a New York City sidewalk, the doctor in a desperate attempt to inject life into my corpse. The platelets low the life refusing to coagulate, the blood running loose in bed captured and tied down to the life line of the rwino intravenous tube.
 The T.V. in Law and Order crime scene, crime and blood uninterested from each other, and right there the touch of my mother's hand descend upon my forehead to see if I have a fever.
 I began a secret long talk with her, maybe understanding her situation when she was a teenager, when her life was spinning out of control. A teen, with an inability to care for herself, with 3 children. Hatred that still continues for years. To move

from anger to acceptance takes a long time.

Feeling alienated from others is a place that is easy to go. And the beat goes on, "I suspect others".

Will anxiety, leaping to confusion, dashing to fear, end up in a strident note of a panic attack?

More important now, as I wait in the hospital bed, is to determine the source of anger, the poison dripping drops of distress and anxiety. And for the first time I contemplate to cut Mom some slack.

I am doing things with a sense of ending.

To Saraswati Rosenberg

From a room painted in lilac hues of insinuating color -like a cave- with only one escape, with a sharp morning light filtering thru the glass of a fake window. I begin to write. This time, a tentative autumn is screaming in orange leaves, I have come from crossing the tracks. Oh, I like the dangerous feeling of the sound of an approaching fantasy train that might take my life away. And I can see the poor engineer, full of agony in a cascade of "I don't know where she came from, and when I saw her it was too late, I applied the brakes, but that also was too late!" And I, angelical and beautiful in a Law-

and-Order-kind-of-crime-scene, a tiny river of blood oozing from my parted lips. Oh! Suicide, yes! I have come to write in silence, full of light and the color opens itself to my friend in transgressions, my name in other languages, a mirror reflecting a shadow of a drifter passing by, and a beggar that lives from the public display of the charity of others that is difficult to speak of.

The blood work of the crime scene

Patient sounds like *patience*. Patience I have to have in profusion for the curious medical students asking the same parade of questions until I repeat so many times the epic drama of the distorted image of myself that I get bored, and a sense of detachment surfaces and it is not about me, me, me that I am talking answering questions about this limping middle aged woman, pinned down in a life of common place story being her best own victim. Compliance is the key, complying at each step along the way to nail one more nail in the coffin of the hospital bed, because compliance is the key and refusing to cooperate will put me on the wrong side of town with the extreme lunatic and "non compliant will be written in my medical chart.

ENTHUSIASTIC

CONFIDENT

The future arrives organized and efficient.

Diagnosis

Our psychological and emotional selves are strained to the breaking point.

Visits to the Puzzle

In the waiting room, in front of the sacrificial chair where I give blood to a crystal tube of uncertainties, and received a warm smile of Olatunye, the nurse with cotton fingers. The combination of smile and cotton fingers, an open space of confidence, a secure sense of being taking care of, and it is not the super modern new medical file records system that the administration is installing now, for us to be able to access our record from any place in a blink of an eye, so that we can access our detailed miseries from home, and relish in the ups and down of the spiral of my illness; truly does not put me at ease.

And I see her moving slow, taking hold of the tube –already full of surprisingly obscure red blood, quasi black– and in a sweep of sweetness, places it in front of my haunted eyes. The tube of blood, culprit of my sorrow, the essence of the unbalanced, the body of malady for me to see, and her voice is a sincere sound of steady tranquility saying –"Is this your name?"

But I know the drama of many names. Yes, right there, in such a simple question –What is my name? – A rollercoaster spinning, spitting the joke of a parade of names. Marcia, Catalina, Cathy, Catherine, Marcia Catalina, Sister Maitreyi, and the other ones, like Ratona, Gallinita-de-media-libra; and Mama-deo-culebra-se-tira-un peo-culebra. Which one to choose this time?

Not to mention the last name! Writing Matos one semester in the front page of text books, to be changed in the next semester, depending on my mother's latest drama with my real father or my stepfather, like the game musical chairs.

Don't forget Sister Maitreyi Chaitanya, Maitreyi Villamán. Maitreyi Villamán Matos.

Then again a hesitation comes back, which one should I use? Is it appropriate to be called Sister Maitreyi Villamán? Maitreyi Villamán? Again, and again, and again. The name, the identity, the who i am, the I. The sticker on the crystal tube revealing the sick blood, chanting the name Marcia Catalina Villamán, the one chosen by my father, brings me out from a second of partial distraction, or the condescending drama of my life, the name game.

–Yes, for short, is my answer.

Experiences with the illness

Dealing with a chronic, recurrent thought: "let it make you a victim"

Find myself without hope.

Be prepared to deal with a helping of depression, A Survivor speak!

> The greatest gift that has come my way is that of time. Time to reflect upon!

What the doctor doesn't say is that my life will never be the same, like dropping a stone into a pond.

BEING ANGRY WITH GOD

IS

DANGEROUS
GAME

Embrace the cold,

give up hope,

epic drama waits for tragedy

The cold epic drama has a recurring theme of self-sabotage, giving up hope, waiting for a tragedy to strike me down, in a red alert code, beating of the heart, panning the reality, the eyes are expert in embracing the cold hopelessness of the pity that is beyond help, the heartbreak, epic drama of the quest, ready to rob me of my destiny.

Combining Science & Humanity

isolation

Why me?

Give up!

Unusual irritability
and anger

The need for understanding

Difficulty making decisions

Silent assassin, feeling overwhelmed by fears, panic, dread, worthlessness

Me?

Just Being Present!

Morning reflection

To fill someone else's bucket for the right reason, not out of fear of loneliness, or waiting to manipulate for some love and appreciation, or get a bit of acknowledgment, fishing for some approval because I don't appreciate myself.

To fill some else's bucket out of confidence and love, not out of a sense of lacking, to fill someone's bucket out of the abundance of my over flowing cup of love and then there will be no consequences if I dip into your smile to get myself a little sunshine!

The future revealed

When the drip of Riwno start to burn the skin around the entrance of the IV needle, the future marches in front of me like a parade of medical students to examine your life, writing in the medical chart, and my favorite song and dance in front of La Perla in the Old San Juan, in Puerto Rico can be reduced to a diagnosis of terminal illness, a blood that has renounced the process of coagulation and abandoned itself to run, run wild without restraint, flooding into the wrong spaces. I am without a barrier to contain it. My blood accuses me of running wild, Running back to the narrow streets of La

Caleta, to melt in the sunset in San Juan Bay, jumping to the cruise ship of my future revealed in the tiny drop of the medicine. I would also like to write in my medical chart a new story, and draw the sound of the ocean in Cascajo Beach, the sand glittering, the mirror of the moon, the pain of the needle under my skin imposes a lack, not one moment to alleviate the sting of the metal flavoring in the vein, now that my future is revealed in the tiny drop of medication… in bed, looking.

NOW WHAT?

Hope is a strange invention/ a patent of the heart/ in unremitting action/ yet never wearing out.
      Emily Dickinson

FLIGHT X-ray of Good Medicine

Tackling the emotional side of

Gaining the strength to deal with.

Invest in imagination.

Now is a good time to trust!

The desire to live can overcome a lot of obstacles.

It's true, the evidence keeps getting stronger

Set yourself free!

On describing a picture

To spread the wings of change over the day to day reality of a long time sitting in the waiting room, the hospital is now almost my second home and I have to open my heart to the conversation of my fellows, waiting for the voice calling people's names to go to the blood room. It is the stretching of the arm, reaching with energy to an unknown destiny that can be touched with the fingertips and the face lifts to a gentle sky that is open and spacious. Dr. Judith Richard came to let me know that I would be waiting here for a while. She is full of an aura of youthful hope, and health, and optimism. I felt it was genuine, that she is pouring out that same energy on her patients, and it's because of her heart we are getting better, because she cares.

To Minister Maria Howard, to Mary Rafaly, and to Maria Franklin

A flower in your smile,

And three Mary's to protect me.

To the right and to the left, and to the center,

Crowning flowers adorn the altar

In the color of love.

The center of the labyrinth is to be bold, dressed in the holy armor, forged in the fire of the Word, declaring that it is not yet a weapon that can penetrate this invincible armor created by the story of my ancestors, a long line of blood going back to the beginning of time. I said in a voice of thunder, striking deep in the heart of the forest. To be bold is to be dancing to the sound of the drum. Courageous, intrepid, impulsive, lighting striking down here or there in that eternal sense of daring the danger, to look right into the eye of the storm, standing resolve of antagonism, with a balance of opposites in the head and the feet touching the earth, propelling long roots, stable. Feet standing ready in the midnight hour of the soul, to continue the journey, seeking to arrive at the center of the labyrinth!

In the play *A Streetcar Named Desire* by Tennessee Williams, Stanley Kowalski had Blanche Dubois committed to a mental institution. At the closing moments, Blanche utters her signature line to the kindly doctor who leads her away:

"Whoever you are, I have always depended on the kindness of strangers."

I am very grateful to the following individuals and organization's personnel in Charlottesville, VA for their services render to me with all love and kindness.

Minister Maria Howard, Paola White, Chanel Wilson, and Mary Ann Jackson, from Women of Restoration.

Rev. Kenneth Jones.

Maria Franklin from Women's Initiative.

Meghan Chapman, and Hannah Green from ASG

Deidre Rohan from Focus

Dr. Gregory Townsend, Dr. Ali Esfandiari, Mary L. Rafaly, and D. Bruce Ellsworth Clinical Social Workers UVA; and Kathryn Dort, Barbara Smith from ID Clinic at UVA.

Dr. Gail Macik, Dr. Judith Richard, Dr. John Densmore, and Kelly Davidson from Cancer Center at UVA.

Ashley Short, from Albemarle/Charlottesville Health District Office.

Sandy Walker, Social Services Worker from Salvation Army.

Wanda Rue and Mark Baker from Transformation Retreats.

Herb Dickenson and Christine Colopy from The Heaven.

Tracee James from MACAA

Deborah McLeod from Chroma Projects.

Dr. Margaret DuBose Flather, M.D.

Calvin Tate from Charlottesville Public Access Television

Heather Hightower, Lori Derr, and Beth-Neville Evans, thank you for lending the power of your voices in my first rehearsal for the performance of *Anatomy of an Illness*.

About the author:

Maitreyi Villamán Matos is an accomplished poet, playwright, choreographer, theatre director and producer, born in Dominican Republic and educated in Puerto Rico. In 1980 Maitreyi founded the non-for profit Centro Creativo-Experimental Inarú. Through Inarú, Maitreyi promotes theatre and supports the development of new actors and dramatists, as well as training children in the performing arts. Aside from writing, directing and producing theater, Miss Villamán has conducted and published research on Dominican religious syncretism, the feast of the Holy Cross, yoga and Hindu rituals. To promote and nurture the love of poetry, Maitreyi conducts her signature workshops *Tú Eres Poeta*© - You are a Poet- designed to teach and engage participants from any walk of life to express their poetic voices. The poems written on these workshops are then published as a collection tittled *Tú Eres Poeta*.

Aside from *Anatomy of an Illness*, Maitreyi Villamán Matos has published three books of poetry: *Caso Abierto*; *BX15- A Poetic Journey*, and *El Silencio de los Inocentes*.

La Maga Press/Facebook

New York

Virginia

www.ingramcontent.com/pod-product-compliance
Lightning Source LLC
Chambersburg PA
CBHW072017060426
42446CB00043B/2638